CREATE A CASTLE
AND OTHER GREAT LEGO® IDEAS

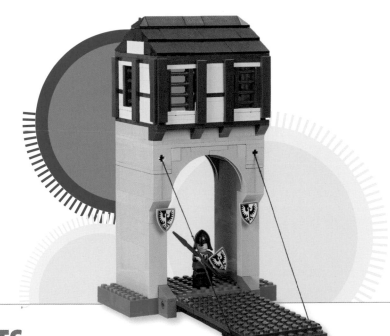

CONTENTS

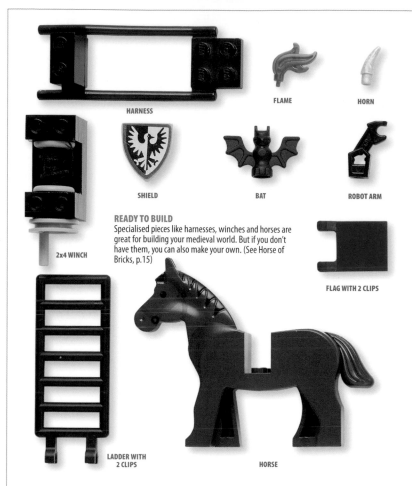

HARNESS

FLAME

HORN

SHIELD

BAT

ROBOT ARM

2x4 WINCH

READY TO BUILD
Specialised pieces like harnesses, winches and horses are great for building your medieval world. But if you don't have them, you can also make your own. (See Horse of Bricks, p.15)

FLAG WITH 2 CLIPS

MEDIUM WAGON WHEEL

BIONICLE® SHIELD

TUBE

LADDER WITH 2 CLIPS

HORSE

MIX AND MATCH
Use pieces from all your LEGO sets to build your medieval scenes – don't just stick to LEGO® Castle sets!

PLANT

STREAMER

LONG CHAIN

SEAT

PIECES OF HISTORY

Who needs a time machine when you can build your own medieval models? Search your LEGO® collection for wheels, weapons and chains. Brown and grey pieces make good wooden or stone structures, while LEGO® Technic parts can help create working mechanisms. Here are some pieces that might come in useful – what else can you find?

4x8 DOOR

4x6x3 ROLLCAGE

TAIL

TORCH

SWORD

SPEAR

LANCE

MEDIEVAL WEAPONRY
Your minifigures can wield weapons – or you could incorporate them into your models as traps or defensive features. (See Siege Tower, p.23)

2x2 ROUND BRICK

2x2 ROUND PLATE

SMALL NARROW RIMS AND 2x2 AXLE PLATE WITH 2 PINS

1x1 ROUND PLATE

1x1 ROUND BRICK

CRANK

LEGO TECHNIC RIGHT ANGLE AXLE CONNECTOR

LEGO TECHNIC LIFT ARM

2x2 DOMED BRICK

1x2x2 ARCHED WINDOW

1x1 SLOPE

1x1 CONE

LEGO TECHNIC
LEGO Technic pieces can make wheels turn, cannons tilt and drawbridges drop. (See Crank Drawbridge, p.6)

1x2 TEXTURED BRICK

1x4 PANEL

2x4 RIDGED ROOF SLOPE

COMPLETE CASTLES
Roof pieces, cones and slopes can add the perfect finishing touch to your castles.

LEGO TECHNIC CROSS AXLE 8

2x2 PLATE WITH 2 RINGS UNDERNEATH

LEGO TECHNIC AXLE CONNECTOR

1x2 JUMPER PLATE

1x1 BRICK WITH 4 SIDE STUDS

LEGO TECHNIC 12 TOOTH GEAR

1x1 BRICK WITH HOLE

LEGO TECHNIC HALF PIN

1x2 BRICK WITH HOLE

1x2 BRICK WITH CROSS AXLE HOLE

1x6 TILE

2x2 TILE

1x2x3 SLOPE

4x4 ROUND BRICK

1x1 PLATE WITH SIDE RING

1x1x6 ROUND COLUMN

2x16 ANGLED SLOPE

2x4 ANGLED PLATE

2x2 CORNER PLATE

2x2 TURNTABLE

1x2/2x2 ANGLE PLATE

4x4 PLATE

2x2 INVERTED SLOPE

1x2 PLATE WITH HANDLED BAR

1x2 PLATE WITH CLICK HINGE

1x1 HEADLIGHT BRICK

1x3x2 HALF ARCH

1x2 LOG BRICK

1x1x5 BRICK

1x3 ARCH BRICK

MEDIEVAL ARCHES
Arches are a common feature in medieval architecture. Try to use them in your buildings.

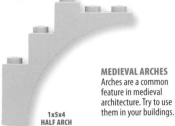
1x5x4 HALF ARCH

1x6 ARCH BRICK

1x4 BRICK WITH SIDE STUDS

1x12 PLATE

1x4 HINGE PLATE AND 4x4 HINGE PLATE

CASTLE

Medieval castles are huge, sturdy structures. Other than that, you can build your model however you want: grand, ornate, plain, strong, majestic or crumbling. You could even build it as a combination of all these things! Look at pictures of ancient castles, or find inspiration in your favourite books and films. Think about including details like flags, wall-mounted torches and knight minifigures to bring your creation to life.

BUILDING BRIEF

Objective: Build medieval castles

Use: Home for royalty and knights, defending the village, location of jewels and treasure

Features: Must be big and strong, able to withstand attack, majestic architecture

Extras: Interior rooms, inner courtyards, drawbridge, moat, gardens, a whole town within the castle walls

CASTLE FORTRESS

Castles are built up over time as each king or queen adds what he or she needs. Start with an impressive doorway and a grand central building. Then add on sections to house sleeping quarters, viewing platforms, dining rooms, chapels, stores and anything else you can think of. They don't even have to match!

Different sections can be built from different materials. Use brown bricks for wooden walls and grey for stone

Log bricks are great for medieval building

ARCHITECTURE

An interesting architectural feature can really give your model a boost. Here, a smaller arch has been built in behind a larger arch, which adds depth and detail to the chapel walls. Cones, round bricks and round plates are stacked to make decorative columns. Be inventive!

Some parts of the castle can be very ornate, even if others are plain. Cones, tiles and side stud pieces can create imposing sculptures

CURVED BATTLEMENTS

Rounded battlements can help your knights keep a lookout in all directions. Use hinged plates to connect several sections of wall together. Then angle the walls into a circle, semicircle or whatever shape you want.

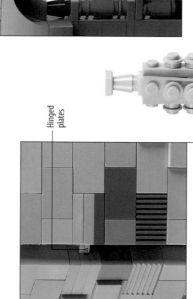

Hinged plates

Fly flags in your army's colours. You could also display shields or printed tiles to identify your king or queen

This castle even has a chapel attached

Arched windows. If you haven't got arched bricks, use half arches or inverted slopes

Arrow slits made from bricks with cross axle holes

A green brick here and there looks like a moss-covered stone!

Bricks in different shades of grey, textured bricks and log bricks help break up large stone walls

Green baseplate is a good starting point, but why don't you try building your castle on a hill, or on an island in the middle of a lake?

Scattered plates and tiles look like fallen ruins

Overgrown foliage suggests an old castle. You could build a well-tended garden instead

Wooden structures with lattice windows look really medieval!

Imposing entrance. You could also add a gatehouse with a way to keep invaders out! (See pp.6–9)

DRAWBRIDGES

Every castle needs protection from invading armies. First build a simple gatehouse as an imposing front to your fortification. Then, think about how best you want to defend your castle and design a mechanism to suit. You could create a portcullis, a heavy stone door or a drawbridge. Here are two clever ways to build a drawbridge!

BUILDING BRIEF
Objective: Build drawbridges for your castle
Use: Protecting the castle's entrance
Features: A mechanism to open and close
Extras: Decorations, guards, defences

Crank controls drawbridge

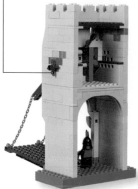
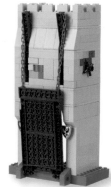

OPEN   **CLOSED**

GATEHOUSE

A simple gatehouse can be the first point of protection for your castle. Grey bricks and LEGO Technic half pins on either side of the door attach the drawbridge.

Make sure the doorway is high enough for a knight to ride through on horseback!

LEGO Technic half pin allows drawbridge to pivot

Push lever to release gears and send drawbridge crashing down!

MEDIEVAL MECHANISM

LEGO Technic gears turn to raise the lift-arms. These pull the chains, raising the drawbridge. A lever secures the drawbridge in place by locking an axle connector against the gears.

CRANK DRAWBRIDGE

A crank system is a simple way to raise and lower a drawbridge. This mechanism is housed in a stone battlement that connects to the top of the gatehouse. It uses LEGO Technic bricks, axles and gears that allow you to operate the drawbridge using a crank on the side of the building.

Make drawbridge wide enough to cover entrance when raised

Drawbridge raised by chains attached to lift-arms

CABLE DRAWBRIDGE

There's more than one way to raise a bridge! This version of the gatehouse uses a spool and string cable system instead of chains and lift-arms. The mechanism is housed in a rustic-style gatehouse room.

CLIPPING THE CABLES

Use plates with handled bars to secure your drawbridge's cables. Thread the cable through both handles before clipping them to the underside of the drawbridge.

Winch

Not enough grey bricks? Build the top of your gatehouse using wood colours instead!

Hand-cranked winch is not as fast as a gear system, but it gets the job done!

SPOOL SYSTEM

The cables are attached to a winch inside the gatehouse, which is turned by a handle on the outside. This system takes up little space, which leaves room in the gatehouse for guards and ammunition.

Use a brick with cross axle hole in it to feed the cables through

CLOSED

Winch

OPEN

Don't have LEGO Technic parts? Use hinged bricks or plates to build a movable drawbridge

Plate with handled bar

PORTCULLIS

A portcullis is a heavy gate that can be raised and lowered on a pulley system. It is another great way to let friends into your castle – and keep enemies out! Start with a simple gatehouse like the one on the previous page, and adjust it to house your portcullis.

AW. THANKS TO THAT PORTCULLIS, WE NEVER GET TO BATTLE ANYBODY ANYMORE!

Put knights and soldiers on top to defend gatehouse

One-brick-wide channel between two layers of the front wall

Tall gatehouse tower leaves room for portcullis to slide all the way up

Decorative windows built with 1x1 round bricks, plates and small arches

GATE GAP

Build two layers into the front wall of the gatehouse, leaving a narrow channel between them. Drop the portcullis into this gap before building the roof, so it is trapped inside the gatehouse, but able to slide up and down freely.

Display your castle's coat of arms on the gatehouse walls. You could also fly flags or hang weapons!

PORTCULLIS

This portcullis is built from crisscrossed long, thin plates, with no special pieces needed. A string attached to a plate with handled bar at the top raises it through a channel created by the space between the two layers of the front walls.

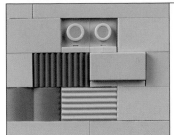

NO ONE GETS IN UNLESS THEY KNOW THE PASSWORD!

BRICKS IN THE WALL

To add realistic textures to a stone wall, include textured bricks and log bricks among regular bricks, or attach 1x2 tiles to pairs of headlight bricks so they protrude from the wall.

When portcullis is closed, brick at end of drawstring sits on top of the tower

Plate with handled bar attaches string to door

To raise gate, pull brick down and attach it to top of archway, holding portcullis in place

REALLY? OK... THE PASSWORD IS "LET ME IN OR ELSE!"

PORTCULLIS LOWERED

You could also put a portcullis behind your castle's front door!

Portcullis moves smoothly because nothing blocks its way

PORTCULLIS RAISED

CASTLE DOORS

When building a door for your castle, think about what it's for. Royal processions and grand entrances? Then make it really big and fancy! To keep out unwanted guests, make it sturdy and strong with a way to lock it from inside. Or perhaps you'd like a secret door to protect a room full of treasure? It's all up to you!

BUILDING BRIEF
Objective: Build doors for your castle
Use: Letting people in, or keeping people out!
Features: Must be able to open and close
Extras: Locks, traps, signs, secret panels

DOOR OF DANGER

The door to a villain's castle should say "keep out!" to any heroes who approach. This simple door is made from standard bricks and tiles and attaches to the frame with clips and handled bars.

A bat or a flaming torch would look just as scary here!

Rattling chain hints at the spooky danger waiting inside

Use pieces with unusual or dramatic shapes to make creepy decorations

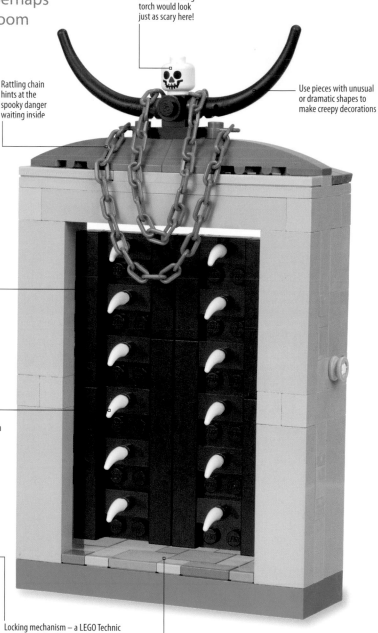

UNHINGED

Build the doors of this creepy entrance first. Next, construct the doorframe around them so you can position the clip pieces correctly.

Horn pieces warn intruders to keep out. You could also use tooth plates or tools

OPEN   **CLOSED**

Locking mechanism – a LEGO Technic cross axle slides through a brick with a hole through it to lock the door

No welcome mat here!

You could add a clip to the front of your doorway to hold a sword, shield or torch that could double up as a secret lever

Old stone walls built with grey bricks of different shapes and shades

SECRET DOOR

The trick to building a secret door is to make it blend in with the castle's wall. First build an arched doorway with two clip plates at the back. Then design your door to match!

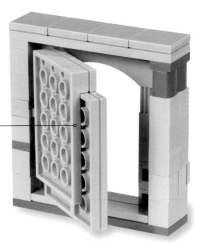

With just a push, the secret passage is revealed

Textured bricks look old and crumbling. Great for a haunted castle!

REAR–OPEN

FRONT–CLOSED

FRONT–OPEN

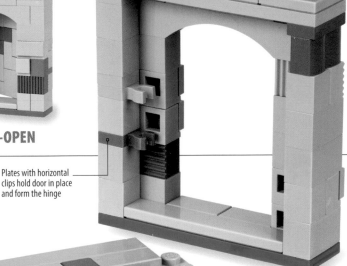

Plates with horizontal clips hold door in place and form the hinge

DOOR DESIGN

Just a few basic plates form the foundation of the door. Cover them with tiles that match the colour and design of the tiles around the doorframe. Now your door will be camouflaged! Make sure there's enough space around the door for it to swing open smoothly.

Plate with handled bar secured with overlapping pieces

TRAPS

To build up your medieval scene, why not add some extra detail to your castle? Perhaps your castle has hidden treasure that needs protecting from thieves. Or maybe you'd rather design a clever way to trap your enemies. Design some sneaky traps to keep your secrets safe! Adding moving parts to your models really brings them to life!

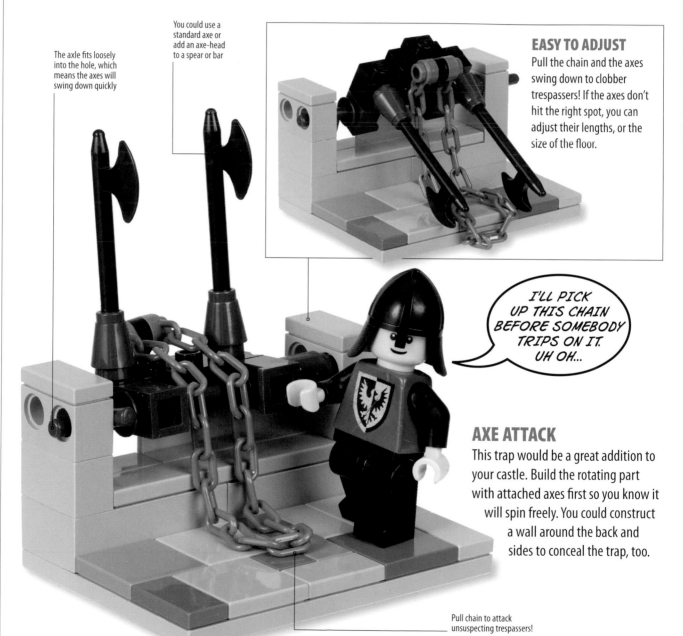

The axle fits loosely into the hole, which means the axes will swing down quickly

You could use a standard axe or add an axe-head to a spear or bar

EASY TO ADJUST

Pull the chain and the axes swing down to clobber trespassers! If the axes don't hit the right spot, you can adjust their lengths, or the size of the floor.

I'LL PICK UP THIS CHAIN BEFORE SOMEBODY TRIPS ON IT. UH OH...

AXE ATTACK

This trap would be a great addition to your castle. Build the rotating part with attached axes first so you know it will spin freely. You could construct a wall around the back and sides to conceal the trap, too.

Pull chain to attack unsuspecting trespassers!

TRAPDOOR

A trapdoor needs to swing down to drop people out of sight, so build it up high. The door should match the rest of the floor (whether wooden or stone) so it's a huge surprise for unsuspecting minifigures!

WHAT A GREAT VIEW. NOW, HOW DO I GET DOWN?

POLES APART
Two lance pieces support the door. One acts as a hinge, while the other can be pulled out to send the door swinging down.

Stopper keeps trap door from swinging too far

Railing – you could also add stairs

Build this platform into your castle's floor to include it in your medieval scene!

Trapdoor built separately from the rest of the platform

Extra piece on end of trap-release pole for better grip

Lance fits loosely in holes so the trap swings open easily

A minifigure who fell through the trap... a long time ago!

KNIGHTLY STEEDS

What's a knight without his faithful horse? On foot, that's what! Many LEGO Castle sets include horses, but you can also build your own. It's simple to give each horse its own individual character! Build and customise special saddles and horse armour, also known as barding. You can even build your knight's armour to match!

Don't have plume pieces? You could use flames, feathers or Viking horns!

NOW THIS IS WHAT I CALL RIDING IN STYLE!

BUILDING BRIEF
Objective: Make horses worthy of a knight!
Use: Riding forth for deeds of derring-do
Features: Must be interesting and colourful
Extras: Coat of arms, plumes, pennants, weapon and shield clips

Helmet has holes for plumes and other decorations

Swap the sword for a lance when it's time for a jousting tournament!

Armour comes in many colours and styles. Choose something that matches your army's colours

Chain makes horse look tough and armoured

You could also add a horse battle helmet to protect your steed

Barding built from angled plates and tiles. Use different plate shapes to create unique saddle designs

MOUNTED KNIGHT

The only buildable surface on a LEGO horse is where the rider's feet attach. So to make your own barding, you'll need to build out from there. Clip and bar plates can help you build in two directions.

Flag pieces make good barding, too!

Use different colours to build up your army's identity

You can use a LEGO saddle or build your own!

MY HORSE IS TOTALLY OFF THE CHAIN!

1x1 plate with horizontal clip

This clips to 1x1 plate with horizontal clip on saddle

A tile locks the plates together without adding too much bulk

Two-toned coat, created by mixing classic and modern brown bricks. Create your own patterns!

Ears made from 1x1 cones

HORSE OF BRICKS

If you don't have a horse for your knight, try building one! This brick-built horse has a gap to fit a minifigure. Its body is built from simple bricks and plates, with a few slopes and inverted slopes.

You could make the bricks around the gap a different colour to resemble a saddle

Hooves made from round black bricks

WAGONS & CARTS

Every medieval villager needs a trusty horse-drawn wagon to get them to the market. Before building your cart or wagon, think about what you want it to carry: food, equipment, passengers? You could even make an armoured battle-wagon with lots of spears and spikes!

Many wagons have smaller front wheels than back wheels

Simple hood shows that driver is a peasant, not a knight or king

BOTTOM VIEW

OFF TO THE MARKET WITH A LOAD OF FRESHLY PICKED BRICKS!

WOODEN WAGON

This wagon has plenty of room for carrying supplies from town to town. Build the part that attaches to the horse first to ensure everything is the right height and all four wheels touch the ground to roll evenly.

Wooden boarding, built from brown tiles. You could use bright colours for a festive painted wagon

Driver's seat stays stationary while front wheels turn

Make sure wheels aren't blocked by back of wagon when it turns

Round brown plate is attached to a turntable, allowing front axle to turn

TURNING THE WAGON

As the horse changes direction, it turns the front axle, which pulls the rest of the wagon along behind. You can use different pieces to make a turning wagon, from a turntable to a LEGO Technic pin.

If you don't have a LEGO horse, try building your own! (See p.15)

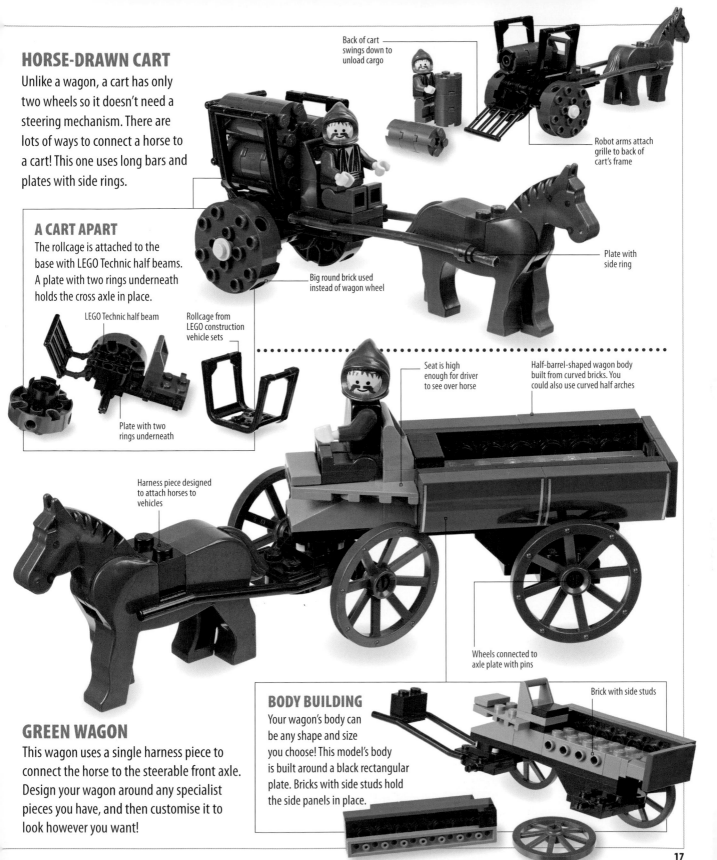

HORSE-DRAWN CART

Unlike a wagon, a cart has only two wheels so it doesn't need a steering mechanism. There are lots of ways to connect a horse to a cart! This one uses long bars and plates with side rings.

Back of cart swings down to unload cargo

Robot arms attach grille to back of cart's frame

A CART APART

The rollcage is attached to the base with LEGO Technic half beams. A plate with two rings underneath holds the cross axle in place.

LEGO Technic half beam

Rollcage from LEGO construction vehicle sets

Plate with two rings underneath

Big round brick used instead of wagon wheel

Plate with side ring

Seat is high enough for driver to see over horse

Half-barrel-shaped wagon body built from curved bricks. You could also use curved half arches

Harness piece designed to attach horses to vehicles

Wheels connected to axle plate with pins

GREEN WAGON

This wagon uses a single harness piece to connect the horse to the steerable front axle. Design your wagon around any specialist pieces you have, and then customise it to look however you want!

BODY BUILDING

Your wagon's body can be any shape and size you choose! This model's body is built around a black rectangular plate. Bricks with side studs hold the side panels in place.

Brick with side studs

DRAGONS

No medieval world is complete without a fierce, fire-breathing dragon. Dragons are mythical creatures, so there are no rules about what they should look like. Give yours spikes, fangs, horns, tails, chains, curves and as many wings as you like! What else can you think of?

FLYING SERPENT

This lean, agile dragon has a twisted body built from lots of LEGO Technic parts. Its back is shaped and held together with ball-and-socket joints, while axles and LEGO Technic half beams make up the front arms.

Don't have these horn pieces? Use screwdrivers, daggers or bars – anything long or pointy will do!

Horns face backward so dragon is streamlined when flying

Neck joint is not fixed in place so the head can be posed as you like

ALL IN HIS HEAD

The dragon's head is built in four different directions. The bottom part has studs facing up, the sloped sides are built outward to the left and right and the inside of the mouth has a jumper plate facing forward, which holds the flame piece in place.

Angle plates allow sideways building

Printed angled slopes add detail

Jumper plate faces forward

Use joints to create posable ankles and knees

Build the shape of your dragon using ball-and-socket joints

I MIGHT BE MADE OF HEAT-RESISTANT PLASTIC, BUT I'M STILL SCARED!

Can your minifigure tame the dragon?

Dragons don't have to have feet! Why not build some claws instead?

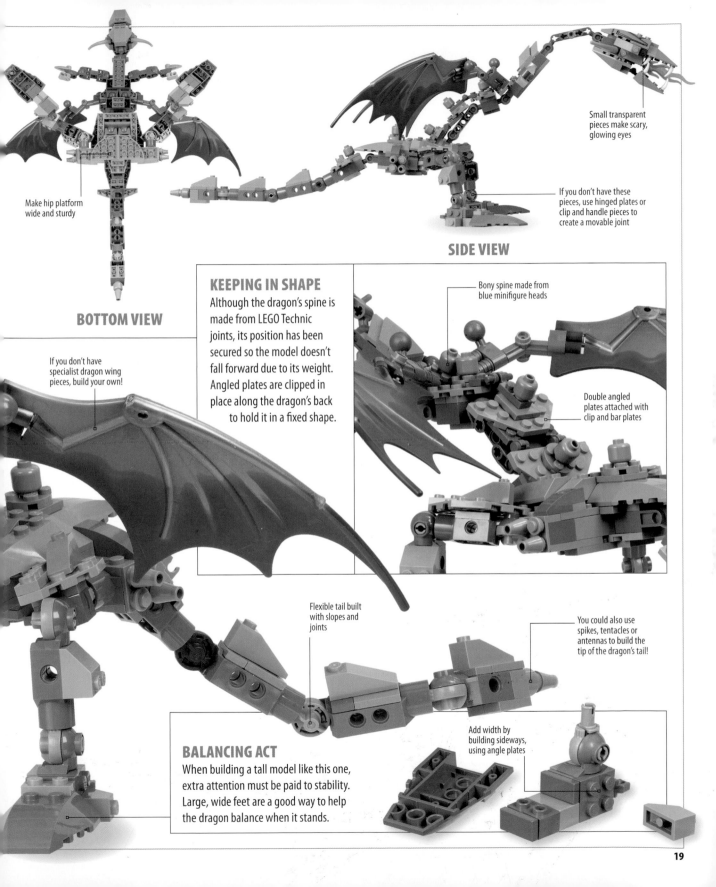

Make hip platform wide and sturdy

Small transparent pieces make scary, glowing eyes

If you don't have these pieces, use hinged plates or clip and handle pieces to create a movable joint

SIDE VIEW

BOTTOM VIEW

If you don't have specialist dragon wing pieces, build your own!

KEEPING IN SHAPE

Although the dragon's spine is made from LEGO Technic joints, its position has been secured so the model doesn't fall forward due to its weight. Angled plates are clipped in place along the dragon's back to hold it in a fixed shape.

Bony spine made from blue minifigure heads

Double angled plates attached with clip and bar plates

Flexible tail built with slopes and joints

You could also use spikes, tentacles or antennas to build the tip of the dragon's tail!

BALANCING ACT

When building a tall model like this one, extra attention must be paid to stability. Large, wide feet are a good way to help the dragon balance when it stands.

Add width by building sideways, using angle plates

BATTERING RAMS

A battering ram is like a medieval tank: heavy, tough and almost unstoppable. It needs a sturdy frame and a strong, swinging ram that can smash through your enemy castle's best defences. It needs a set of wheels too, so your LEGO knights can move the huge contraption around!

BUILDING BRIEF
Objective: Build battering rams
Use: Breaking through the fortifications of enemy castles
Features: Strength, stability, swinging mechanism
Extras: Wheels, shields, armour plates, flags

SWING AND SMASH

A swinging mechanism is built into this ram's support frame. The castle's attackers stand behind the ram, pull it back as far as they can and then let go. Gravity and momentum take care of the rest!

Axles at the top and bottom of the lift arms let battering ram swing back and forth freely

Battering ram hangs from two pairs of LEGO Technic lift arms

You could also use wagon wheels for a lighter, faster battering ram

Swinging hinge made from LEGO Technic cross axle and bricks with holes

Make the frame as sturdy as you can with overlapping bricks

Angle plates attach sides to the base

I LOVE THE SOUND OF CASTLE GATES CRASHING DOWN IN THE MORNING!

Silver plates look like bolted metal to hold heavy loads

REAR SIDE VIEW

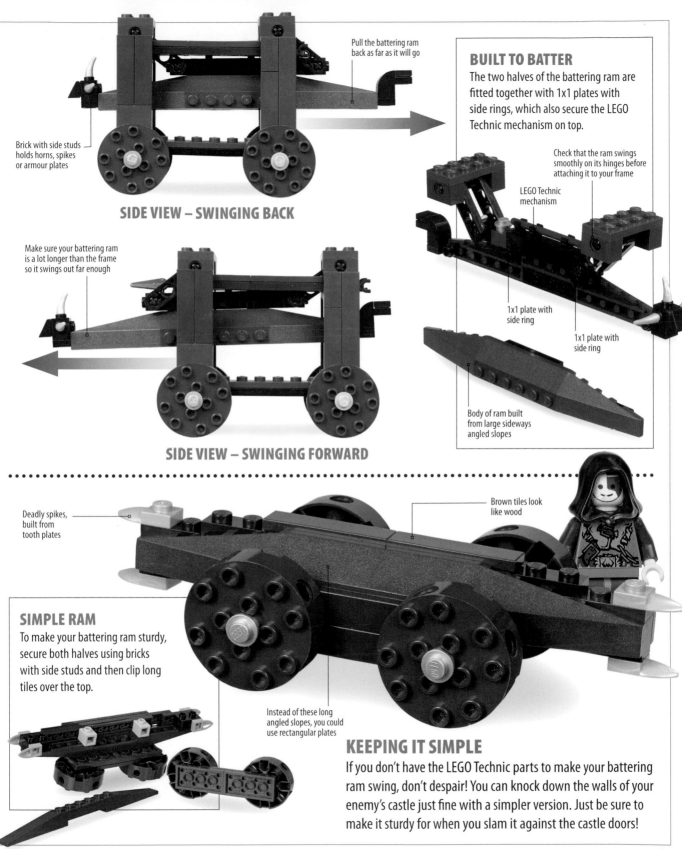

Pull the battering ram back as far as it will go

Brick with side studs holds horns, spikes or armour plates

SIDE VIEW – SWINGING BACK

Make sure your battering ram is a lot longer than the frame so it swings out far enough

SIDE VIEW – SWINGING FORWARD

BUILT TO BATTER

The two halves of the battering ram are fitted together with 1x1 plates with side rings, which also secure the LEGO Technic mechanism on top.

Check that the ram swings smoothly on its hinges before attaching it to your frame

LEGO Technic mechanism

1x1 plate with side ring

1x1 plate with side ring

Body of ram built from large sideways angled slopes

Deadly spikes, built from tooth plates

Brown tiles look like wood

SIMPLE RAM

To make your battering ram sturdy, secure both halves using bricks with side studs and then clip long tiles over the top.

Instead of these long angled slopes, you could use rectangular plates

KEEPING IT SIMPLE

If you don't have the LEGO Technic parts to make your battering ram swing, don't despair! You can knock down the walls of your enemy's castle just fine with a simpler version. Just be sure to make it sturdy for when you slam it against the castle doors!

LAYING SIEGE

Laying siege to an enemy castle is no easy task! You can build all kinds of equipment for your army of knights. A portable shield will protect them from spears and arrows as they advance across the battlefield, while a tall siege tower will help them climb over the castle walls.

BUILDING BRIEF
Objective: Build siege equipment
Use: Reaching and getting into enemy castles
Features: Must be portable and arrow-proof
Extras: Mounted crossbows, flags, shields

Use grey bricks to create a stone wall – but remember, a stone wall wouldn't be portable!

Cones at top create the look of wooden poles bound together

PORTABLE SHIELD

Offering protection for knights on the move, this shield wall is made by alternating 1x2 log bricks with 1x1 round bricks. This structure makes the wall flexible enough to bend into a curve.

IT'S LIKE A GAME OF HIDE AND GO SEEK... READY OR NOT, HERE WE COME!

Siege army is safe and sound behind the wall!

Rolling wheel rims allow knights to push wall toward castle

Plate with click hinge

ROLLING WALL

The portable shield rolls on small wheel rims without tyres. You can attach a horse to the click hinge at the front to tow the wall to the battlefield!

Wheel rim

REAR VIEW

SIEGE TOWER

A siege tower is like an armoured ladder for reaching the top of enemy walls. This one is built on a rectangular plate and has a drawbridge-like gangplank to deposit the knights onto castle walls.

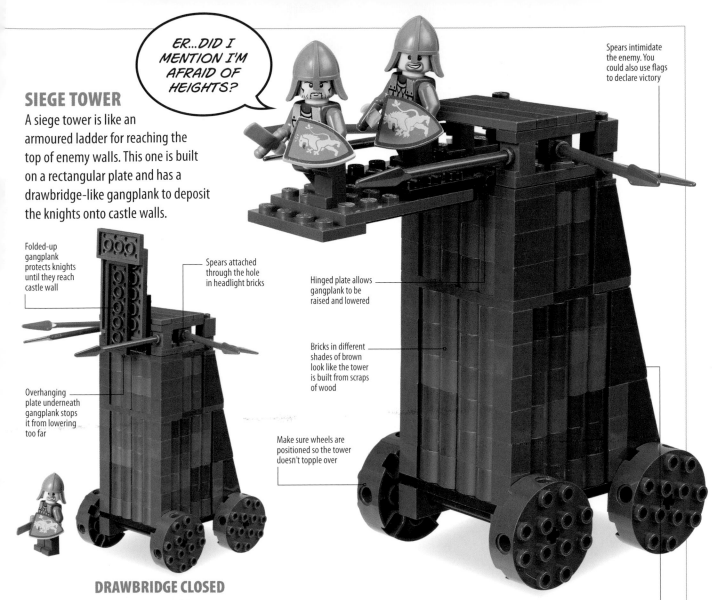

ER...DID I MENTION I'M AFRAID OF HEIGHTS?

Spears intimidate the enemy. You could also use flags to declare victory

Folded-up gangplank protects knights until they reach castle wall

Spears attached through the hole in headlight bricks

Hinged plate allows gangplank to be raised and lowered

Bricks in different shades of brown look like the tower is built from scraps of wood

Overhanging plate underneath gangplank stops it from lowering too far

Make sure wheels are positioned so the tower doesn't topple over

DRAWBRIDGE CLOSED

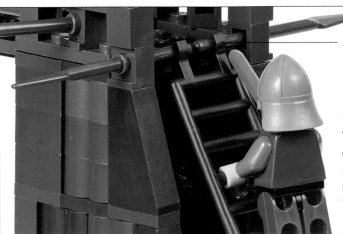

Knights climb up ladder or take shelter inside open back of tower

HOLLOW INSIDE

The back of the siege tower is left open so that the knights can hide inside. A ladder is clipped on to two of the side spears. It can be folded out to allow the knights to climb up it.

REAR VIEW

CANNONS & CATAPULTS

Siege weapons are designed to throw objects at or over a castle's walls. Beyond that, the only limit is your imagination! So be creative and keep an eye out for parts that would work as catapult buckets or cannon barrels. And remember – don't aim anything at your eyes!

BUILDING BRIEF
- **Objective:** Build siege weapons
- **Use:** Attacking castle walls and towers
- **Features:** Ability to throw, fling or launch projectiles
- **Extras:** Wheels, guards, spare ammo wagons

TILT TO AIM

This cannon can be tilted up and down thanks to a few LEGO Technic pieces. The barrel is built around two bricks with holes, through which is fitted a cross axle.

Axle allows cannon to tilt

Brick with a hole

Barrel made from 2x2 round bricks with a domed brick at the back

Frame uses LEGO Technic parts so the barrel can move up and down

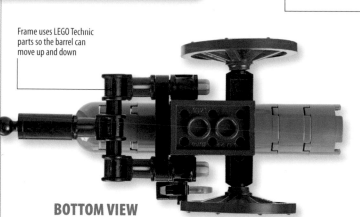

BOTTOM VIEW

MICROCATAPULT

The basic components of a catapult are a bucket attached to an arm and a sturdy base to support them. With a rotation point in the middle of the throwing arm, this catapult works like a see-saw.

Rotation point

Radar dish for bucket

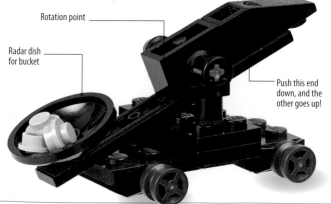

Push this end down, and the other goes up!

Wagon wheels make a heavy cannon more portable

MICROCANNON

For a siege on a smaller scale, you can make a microcannon. This model is built out of two LEGO Technic tubes, supported by headlight bricks.

ASSEMBLE YOUR WEAPONS!

The LEGO Technic tubes are connected by a plate with horizontal clip, which attaches to the headlight bricks with 1x1 round plates.

1x1 round plate

Plate with horizontal clip

Torch made from a flame piece and robot arm

THIS CANNON IS SURE TO GO WITH A BANG!

CANNON

Official LEGO cannons can be found in many ship sets. If you don't have one, though, just build your own! You need a long barrel, a base and some wheels if you want to make it mobile.

MICROMEDIEVAL

Have you ever wanted to build a really big castle, but didn't have enough bricks? Try shrinking it down! Build it at a smaller-than-minifigure scale to make huge structures from just a few bricks. Your LEGO knights might not fit inside, but with the right pieces and some imagination, you can create churches, houses, animals – even a whole micromedieval world!

BUILDING BRIEF
Objective: Build microscale castles and other microcreations
Use: Building up a medieval world
Features: Tiny but easily identifiable
Extras: A whole surrounding kingdom

FANTASY CASTLE

This magical castle may be small, but it has plenty of interest. A small arch is used to top the front gate, a tile can be a drawbridge, and round 1x1 bricks make the towers. The roofs are covered in 1x1 dark grey slopes, cones and tiles to complement the sand-coloured walls.

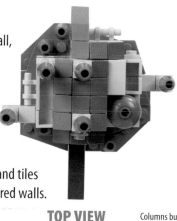

TOP VIEW

Make your castle as elaborate as you want!

Columns built with 1x1 round bricks and plates

Drawbridge is a single tile supported by plates

A 1x1 cone makes a great tree at microscale!

Square windows are actually the backs of headlight bricks

Castle roof made from ridged roof slopes

Arched window

STONE CASTLE

For a traditional-looking castle, start with a few plates to make a base. Next, add the corner towers and then build the rest of the castle between them. Pointy roofs, arched doors and thin walls complete the look!

Tree made from 1x1 round brick

TOP SIDE VIEW

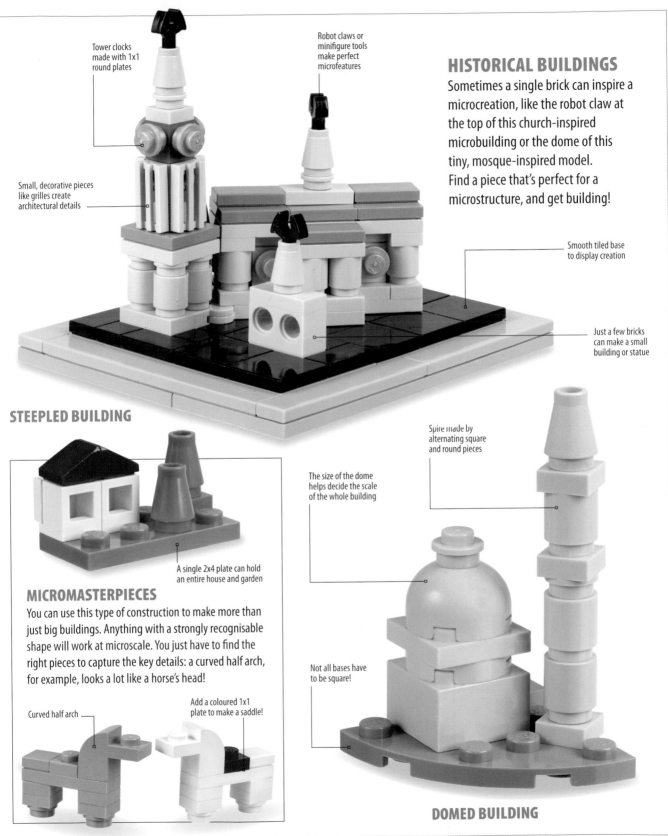

Tower clocks made with 1x1 round plates

Robot claws or minifigure tools make perfect microfeatures

HISTORICAL BUILDINGS

Sometimes a single brick can inspire a microcreation, like the robot claw at the top of this church-inspired microbuilding or the dome of this tiny, mosque-inspired model.
Find a piece that's perfect for a microstructure, and get building!

Small, decorative pieces like grilles create architectural details

Smooth tiled base to display creation

Just a few bricks can make a small building or statue

STEEPLED BUILDING

Spire made by alternating square and round pieces

The size of the dome helps decide the scale of the whole building

A single 2x4 plate can hold an entire house and garden

MICROMASTERPIECES

You can use this type of construction to make more than just big buildings. Anything with a strongly recognisable shape will work at microscale. You just have to find the right pieces to capture the key details: a curved half arch, for example, looks a lot like a horse's head!

Not all bases have to be square!

Curved half arch

Add a coloured 1x1 plate to make a saddle!

DOMED BUILDING

27

MEET THE BUILDER

SEBASTIAAN ARTS

Location: The Netherlands
Age: 27
LEGO Specialty: Castles and other medieval buildings

What are you inspired by?

I mostly make buildings, so I often get inspiration just walking around town. Whenever I watch documentaries or read articles about castles and medieval buildings, my fingers really itch to build! I also get a lot of inspiration from films – I pay particular attention to the background buildings and scenery. Seeing LEGO® creations by other builders is also a great source of inspiration: sometimes I'll see a clever building technique or part of a creation that makes me think, so I can't stop myself from sitting down and building.

Placing part of your building at an unusual angle can really make your castle a lot more interesting looking.

It's not all about castles! You can also build churches, houses and farms in a medieval setting. This model is based on the church of Scherpenheuvel in Belgium.

To the walls! Siege towers like this were used very widely in the Middle Ages. Invaders could approach their enemy's castle walls protected in their siege tower and then use the height of the tower to climb up and over the castle walls.

If you had all the LEGO® bricks (and time!) in the world, what would you build?

NOTHING IS IMPOSSIBLE WITH LEGO BRICKS!

This is a subject that has come up in conversations with other fans many times before, and for me that's an easy answer. There's a castle on a rocky island in the north of France named Mont Saint-Michel. I would love to build that whole castle in full minifigure scale. That would be my dream creation.

What is your favourite creation?

The "Abbey of Saint Rumare", a fictional fortified church built on a rock. It's big, complex and full of different techniques and building styles – the landscape alone combines water with landscaping, rocky surfaces and vegetation. The main structure has a huge church in tan, grey fortifications, and lots of different buildings inside in different colours and styles, to create that messy, thrown-together look that you would often find in medieval castles.

What things have gone wrong and how have you dealt with them?

My first response to any question like this would be that nothing is impossible with LEGO bricks! If you're building something that doesn't quite fit, there's always a different combination of parts that will fit. If you can't figure it out, step back for a bit, do something else and go back to your "problem" later – you'll often suddenly see a solution.

What is the biggest or most complex model you've made?

The biggest model I've made is the "Abbey of Saint Rumare". This model was also quite complex, because everything is built at different angles. My most complex model by far was a star-shaped fort, which I named "Herenbosch". The star shape created a series of odd angles linked together, which then had to fit snugly with the buildings inside the castle. This took a lot of work — mostly trial and error – to find exactly the right angles for every part of the castle.

Height can add another dimension to your creation. A tall castle can look a lot more impressive than a bigger, more spread out one. This is my favourite creation, the Abbey of Saint Rumare.

How old were you when you started using LEGO bricks?

On my fourth birthday I received my first LEGO sets, and it all started there: I got hooked straight away. For every birthday that followed, all I wanted was more LEGO sets. From an early age, I always enjoyed building my own creations.

A drawbridge can also be used as an effective door. However, you need to make it big enough to cover the gate when raised.

What are some of your top LEGO tips?

When building a castle, don't limit yourself to just one or two colours. Real castles often took a long time to build, and sometimes bits were added later with a different material. You should also be open to building in different directions: Don't have enough bricks to build a wall? A plate with tiles on its side makes a perfect wall. Don't have enough tiles to make a smooth floor? Try building a wall and placing it on its side to make the floor.

Do you plan out your build? If so, how?

Yes, definitely. Whenever I have a building in mind, I draw a plan of it first, to determine how big each part of the castle should be compared to the other parts around it. I really love building at odd angles, so this requires quite a bit of measuring before I can even start building. I always get the plan on paper before I start building, that way when I do start building, I know exactly where to begin. Of course, I leave enough room for improvisation – if something doesn't quite fit as planned, or if I suddenly come up with a better idea when I actually have the bricks in my hands. So, even if I have drawn a plan to begin from, I usually change it and improvise while building.

Adding detailed and uneven terrain around your castle looks more realistic and also more dynamic.

Star-shaped forts such as my "Herenbosch" model were very common in the late Middle Ages, after the invention of gunpowder and cannons. The angle of the walls makes it more difficult for cannonballs to punch straight through them.

I OFTEN GET INSPIRATION JUST WALKING AROUND TOWN.

What else do you enjoy making, apart from castles?

I really love everything that I can make with LEGO bricks! I'm mostly into buildings – not just medieval buildings but also more modern town buildings or even science-fiction laboratories or spaceship hangars. Apart from that I also enjoy building cars, spaceships, pirate ships and heavy machinery such as bulldozers or excavators. It really depends what I'm in the mood to build.

Which model were you most proud of as a young LEGO builder?

I was always into castles as a kid, too, so my most fond memories are of the biggest castles I could build. I would use as many of my LEGO pieces as I could to build the biggest possible castle. One castle I can particularly remember being proud of was one that had a big dragon's head as a gate – that was very tricky to make and I thought it looked very real and menacing.

What is your favourite LEGO technique or technique you use the most?

I always love finding new ways to make the same thing, and I love using as many different techniques in the same creation as I can, while still keeping it coherent. What I use the most is the technique of using different-coloured and different-shaped bricks to break up an otherwise boring grey wall. Other than that, I love building at all sorts of odd angles to make any building look more interesting. There are many ways to place things at an angle, and there's really no right or wrong way to do it, as long as your chosen technique achieves the correct angle.

What is your favourite LEGO brick or piece?

That's an easy choice for me: the headlight brick.

How much time do you spend building?

This really depends on how inspired I am. Sometimes, I don't build at all for a few weeks. But sometimes, when I have an idea in my head I just can't stop building, and I build from the moment I get home from work until the moment I get so tired that I just have to go to bed.

Don't have enough bricks of the same colour? You can always combine different colours. In this case I used grey for stone and red for clay bricks.

If you build a trapdoor, make sure it looks just like the rest of the floor, so it's not easy to spot

How many LEGO bricks do you have?

I don't know the exact number, because I buy bricks in bulk and trade bricks with other LEGO fans. However, based on other people's collections and logical guesswork, I estimate my collection at about 700,000-750,000 pieces.

Penguin Random House

Senior Editor Laura Gilbert
Editors Jo Casey, Hannah Dolan, Emma Grange, Shari Last, Catherine Saunders, Lisa Stock, Victoria Taylor, Natalie Edwards, Matt Jones, Helen Leech, Clare Millar, Rosie Peet
Senior Cover Designer Mark Penfound
Senior Designers Nathan Martin, David McDonald, Anthony Limerick
Designers Owen Bennett, Lynne Moulding, Robert Perry, Lisa Sodeau, Ron Stobbart, Rhys Thomas, Toby Truphet, Thelma Jane-Robb, Gema Salamanca, Abi Wright
Pre-Production Producer Kavita Varma
Senior Producer Kathleen McNally
Managing Editor Paula Regan
Design Managers Jo Connor, Guy Harvey
Creative Manager Sarah Harland
Publisher Julie Ferris
Art Director Lisa Lanzarini
Publishing Director Simon Beecroft

Photography by Gary Ombler,
Brian Poulsen and Tim Trøjborg

Acknowledgements
Dorling Kindersley would like to thank: Stephanie Lawrence, Randi Sørensen and Corinna van Delden at the LEGO Group; Sebastiaan Arts, Tim Goddard, Deborah Higdon, Barney Main, Duncan Titmarsh (www.bright-bricks.com) and Andrew Walker for their amazing models; Jeff van Winden for additional building; Daniel Lipkowitz for his fantastic text; Gary Ombler, Brian Poulsen and Tim Trøjborg for their brilliant photography; Rachel Peng and Bo Wei at IM Studios.

First published in Great Britain in 2017 by
Dorling Kindersley Limited 80 Strand, London, WC2R 0RL

Contains material previously published in
The LEGO® *Ideas Book* (2011)

001-310861-Oct/17

A CIP catalogue record for this book is available from the British Library.

ISBN: 978-0-2413-3047-0
Printed in China.
www.dk.com
www.LEGO.com

A WORLD OF IDEAS:
SEE ALL THERE IS TO KNOW